The Official
Hibernian
Football Club
Annual 2007

Written by David Forsyth

A Grange Publication

Contents

Introduction 7
Manager Profile 8
Season Review 10
Quiz of the Season 23
Rob Jones 24
Eddie Turnbull 26
Training Ground 30
Player Profiles 32
Club History and Honours 44
Know Your History? 46
Merouane Zemmama 49
Magic Moment 49
History Quiz 50
Nickname Quiz 51
Hibs Kids 52
Intertoto Cup 53
Academy - Two to Watch 54
Celebrity Fans 56
Skipper Talks 58
Quiz Answers 60

www.hibernianfc.co.uk

Introduction

Welcome to the Hibernian FC Official 2007 Annual.

Profiles of the Squad, a chat with Manager Tony Mowbray, a review of last season month by month, a profile of Hibernian legend Eddie Turnbull, quizzes, and a snapshot of some of our league-winning seasons are all included in this edition.

We also take a look at some young players to watch for the future, discover the passion of one or two celebrity fans and look back at a particularly special moment from last season.

We hope you enjoy the annual, and remember – **Glory, glory to the Hibees!**

Manager Profile

He is the man behind the free-flowing, attacking football that has seen fans return to Easter Road.

But there's more to the Tony Mowbray philosophy on football than simply a manager who loves his teams to play passing, exciting football.

The Manager of Hibernian FC is renowned as one of the game's deepest thinkers, and as a man worth listening to. So when he lays out his vision for the football club, you can be sure it has been carefully thought through.

Tony is a genuine believer in football clubs retaining their own identity through close links with their community, and through the nurturing and production of their own talent. He said:

"I believe that every football club should have an identity and you have to stamp your mark on that identity. Players come and go, managers come and go but whilst they are in place they have a responsibility to follow the philosophy that they believe in."

Tony is in little doubt of the fans view at Easter Road.

"I've tried to look at the history of the football club and tried to see what it's about and – as with West Ham United or Tottenham Hotspur or Ipswich Town – this is a Club where the supporters want to see a particular brand of passing football.

"You hope it is a winning brand, of course, but I think Hibernian fans want to see young players who have a feeling for the Club try to do the right things every week."

A major plus for the Manager over the past year has been the announcement that the Club has secured land on which to develop a top quality training facility in East Lothian – something he has long listed as a top priority.

He said: **"Having the training centre is very important to the future of this Club in all kinds of ways – from showing around potential new players right through to persuading parents that their kids should sign up with this Club as one that will ensure everything is done for their development."**

JULY 2005

The season kicked off with an eagerly awaited pre-season tour to Ireland, well attended by fans. Three games were played – a thrilling 3-3 draw with Cork City, a 5-0 hammering of St Patricks and a hard fought 1-1 draw with Shamrock Rovers. Other pre-season friendlies included a 4-1 defeat of Berwick Rangers, a 2-0 win against Stirling Albion and a 1-1 draw at Ayr United. The team then travelled to play German side Rot-Weiss Essen to mark the 50th anniversary of the Club making history against the same opposition as the first British side to play in Europe, and again Hibernian came out on top with a 3-0 win. A 1-0 home win against Hartlepool followed before the SPL season kicked off in earnest at Easter Road on July 30th with a 1-1 draw which saw Scott Brown sent off in the first half after Dunfermline had taken an early lead. A spirited fight back by the ten-man Hibernian saw O'Connor bang home an equaliser.

Season Review 2005-06

AUGUST 2005

The first derby of the season took place at Tynecastle with Hearts starting strongly under new manager George Burley. It was Hearts who started far stronger and took an early lead when Skacel scored in 12 minutes. Hibernian skipper Gary Caldwell had to be replaced for a rib and lung injury and Hearts added three second half goals to win the game 4-0.

As was to happen throughout the season, the team showed its mettle in bouncing back from adversity. Livingston were next up at Easter Road, and goals from Murphy, Shiels and O'Connor saw Hibernian run out easy 3-0 winners. An away trip to Falkirk, managed by ex-Hibernian star John "Yogi" Hughes saw the Edinburgh side win a good passing game 2-0, and then it was Rangers at Ibrox.

The two sides were locked at 0-0 after an hour, and Tony Mowbray sent on flying Irishman Ivan Sproule for the final half hour. It was a masterstroke, as the winger used his incredible pace to destroy the Rangers team and score a hat-trick in a 3-0 win.

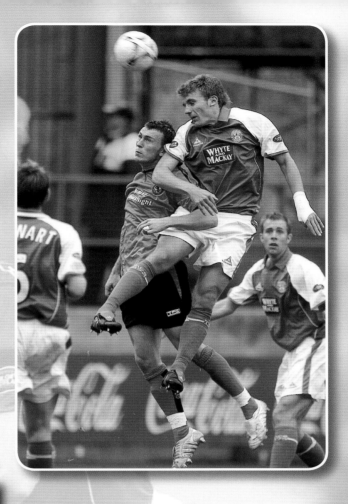

SEPTEMBER 2005

Dundee United were the first visitors to Easter Road during September, bringing with them former Hibernian player Grant Brebner and it was the midfielder who slotted home the first goal after just 14 minutes. However, Hibernian were always in the ascendancy and goals from O'Connor and Sproule saw Hibernian run out 2-1 winners.

Next up was the visit of Ukrainian cracks Dnipro Dnipropetrovsk for a UEFA Cup tie, played before a noisy crowd of almost 17,000. The game ended 0-0 but was as exciting a no-scoring draw as has been seen at Easter Road for sometime. A big game followed in the league, with Celtic visiting Hibernian and – despite being under massive pressure from a pacy Hibernian attack for much of the game the Hoops ran out the narrowest of winners with a goal from Petrov.

An away trip to Ayr United was next up in the CIS Cup, and another tough game saw Hibernian win 2-1 with two goals from Riordan. A 3-1 away win to Motherwell followed, with Beuzelin, Stewart and Riordan all hitting the net. The month ended in the away leg of the UEFA tie at Dnipro. Hibernian ended up on the wrong side of a 5-1 scoreline that hugely flattered the Ukrainian hosts with Hibernian seeing two goals chalked off.

Season Review 2005-06

OCTOBER 2005

First up in October was a home match against Inverness, who were to prove awkward opponents for Hibernian throughout the season. The first match ended in a 2-1 loss, with Steven Fletcher scoring the only Hibernian goal of the game. A friendly away to Irish side Institute – from whom the club had signed Ivan Sproule – followed with Hibernian recording a 2-2 draw, but it was back to winning ways at Easter Road thereafter with a thrilling 4-2 win against Kilmarnock which saw Hibernian come storming back from a half-time 0-2 deficit with goals from Caldwell, Beuzelin (2) and Riordan in one of the finest fight backs seen at Easter Road for many a year. Aberdeen on the road was next up, and Hibernian found it tough against the Dons but came away with all three points following a Derek Riordan strike, and then two from O'Connor saw Hibernian beat Dunfermline 2-1 in Fife.

Next up were derby rivals Hearts at Easter Road, and the chance to avenge the early season beating at Tynecastle. Hearts arrived with John McGlynn at the helm following the departure of George Burley and the game started in typical, electric derby fashion. However on this occasion it was Hibernian who dominated and two strikes in the last 25 minutes following the sending off of Hearts striker Edgaras Jankauskas ensured the points and the bragging rights stayed in Leith.

NOVEMBER 2005

An away trip to Livingston was first up for Tony Mowbray's men and a 2-1 win was achieved with goals from Shiels and O'Connor. The month saw one of the genuine low points of the season with a 3-0 away defeat to struggling Dunfermline in the CIS Cup seeing Hibernian crash out in the quarter final of the competition. Further agony was to follow, as Hibernian entertained Falkirk at Easter Road and threw away a 2-0 half-time lead to succumb 3-2 – much to the disappointment of manager Tony Mowbray. Derek Riordan scored both for Hibernian. Rangers were the next visitors to Easter Road, still smarting from the 3-0 mauling at Ibrox and determined to gain revenge. It wasn't to be, with a fantastic Hibernian performance – especially in a sublime first half in which Hibernian led through goals by Riordan and O'Connor – being rewarded with a 2-1 win against the Glasgow giants. Rangers manager Alex McLeish said after the match that Hibernian's first half performance was "the best football any team has played against us."

Season Review 2005-06

DECEMBER 2005

On paper December looked a tough month, with three of the four fixtures falling away from home and so it was to prove.

Dundee United took full advantage of some uncharacteristically poor Hibernian finishing to score and take an undeserved 1-0 win and all three points, and then Hibernian travelled to Parkhead to face a powerful Celtic side before a packed house. The game proved a thriller, with Hibernian a goal down at half time and then coming out and performing brilliantly in the second-half to storm into a 2-1 lead with goals from Beuzelin and a belter from Fletcher. Then it was the turn of Celtic to storm back with two goals to lead 3-2 and, while the game swung one way and then another, that is how the match ended. Motherwell were the only visitors to Easter Road during the month, and the team duly took advantage with a 2-1 win through Fletcher and Riordan that delivered the points before the month ended with a visit to Inverness in the Highlands which brought a 2-0 defeat.

JANUARY 2006

Hibernian started the month with only their second draw of the campaign, with the honours shared in a pulsating 2-2 encounter against Kilmarnock at Rugby Park. Hibernian had gone behind only to level through Chris Hogg and then appear to win the game through O'Connor until Killie equalised deep into injury time. The Scottish Cup was next on the menu, with a home tie against Arbroath seeing Hibernian record a stunning 6-0 win through Brown (2), Sproule, Stewart, O'Connor and Fletcher. Aberdeen were the visitors to Easter Road on SPL business next, and – despite a Steven Whittaker strike – the Dons ran out 2-1 winners in a match which had seen some catastrophic early defending from the home side concede two soft goals. Dogged defending in the face of an attacking onslaught saw the Dons take advantage of the gifts they had been presented with. Dunfermline were next up in Leith, and it was back to winning ways with two from Riordan and a Fletcher strike sealing the points in a 3-1 win. The month ended with another visit to Tynecastle. The derby ended in another big loss, with Hibernian going down 4-1 despite enjoying periods of control and some decent play. O'Connor's goal was the only solace for those from the green-and-white side of the city.

Season Review 2005-06

FEBRUARY 2006

The defeat to Hearts in the derby was followed by a difficult Scottish Cup away tie at Rangers. Despite two earlier league wins against the 'Gers, Hibernian travelled to Ibrox as underdogs. Manager Tony Mowbray again called his tactics spot on, with a strong defensive performance taking the sting from Rangers and pace on the counter delivering goals from O'Connor, Sproule and new signing Chris Killen for another historic 3-0 win. The euphoria was carried in to the next SPL match, where Livingston were the unfortunate victims at Easter Road as Hibernian put on a dazzling display to record a 7-0 win through Killen, Riordan (2), O'Connor, Fletcher (2) and an OG. A 0-0 draw away to Falkirk was followed by another match at Rangers on league business, but – perhaps inevitably – this time it was the Ibrox side who ran out winners 2-0. The month ended with an away quarter final in the Scottish Cup against Falkirk. The tightness of earlier encounters with John Hughes' team suggested a close fought tie but Hibernian were to prove this theory wrong with a convincing 5-1 win through Riordan, O'Connor, Sproule, Caldwell and Fletcher.

19

Season Review 2005-06

MARCH 2006

A home debut for Paul Dalglish was marked with a fine 3-1 win against Dundee United in front of 16,000 fans who watched as Hibernian went for the jugular, securing a 3-0 half-time lead. Scorers were Riordan, an OG and Chris Killen. Celtic away at Parkhead was next and the team's good form continued with a Riordan free-kick gaining the lead. However, Celtic equalised before half-time and half-way into the second half took the decisive lead. Motherwell away delivered another thrilling draw, with goals from Killen and Glass earning the Hibees a share of the spoils. Again Hibernian had fought back from a half-time deficit of 0-1 to lead, only to see their opponents snatch an injury time equaliser that, on balance, delivered a fair result. The month ended with another unhappy encounter with Inverness, Hibernian losing 2-0. It was to prove to be the last match against the Highlanders, with Hibernian losing all three encounters of the season.

APRIL 2006

The penultimate month of the season kicked-off in spectacular style, with perhaps the most eagerly awaited Edinburgh derby in decades. Hibernian v Hearts in the semi-final of the Scottish Cup with the winner certain to start the final against Gretna or Dundee as strong favourites was a mouth-watering prospect.

Sadly for all Hibees, the event was to prove a difficult affair. Wracked by injuries, Hibernian were unable to field anything approaching their strongest side, while Hearts were at virtual full strength. Despite this, Hibernian's makeshift side started the brighter and enjoyed the better chances in the opening exchanges until a lightning break after half an hour saw Hearts take the lead. The Tynecastle men then took advantage of individual errors to storm into an unassailable lead, and ultimately ran out comfortable 4-0 winners.

High-flying Kilmarnock were next up, at Easter Road, and Hibernian did well to again bounce back and record a 2-1 win despite a crippling injury list that threatened to see the season fizzle out in disappointment. A 0-1 loss on the road to Aberdeen was followed by a creditable 1-1 draw at Parkhead with a Fletcher strike earning a share of the points with Champions elect Celtic. April brought an early opportunity to avenge the Derby semi final defeat, with Hearts visiting Easter Road for the final derby of the season. Still struggling with injuries Hibernian started as underdogs but a skilful and battling performance saw a 2-1 win recorded. The month ended, as it had started, in disappointment and a 4-0 defeat, this time away to Aberdeen.

Season Review 2005-06

MAY 2006

The final month of the season saw Rangers visit Easter Road. An own goal deflected from a 'Gers head from a whipped Riordan free kick was Hibernian's only score in a 2-1 defeat. The season ended in a loss, with Fletcher scoring in a 3-1 defeat at Kilmarnock.

While injuries played a key role in a difficult final few weeks to the season, in particular in decimating the squad ahead of the Cup semi final, the Club achieved a highly creditable fourth place. Only Celtic, Hearts and Rangers finished higher and – but for those injuries – a higher slot might have been secured.

Quiz of the Season

1 How many matches did the Club play on the pre-season tour of Ireland?

2 Which German side provided the opposition when Hibernian became the first British side to play in Europe, and played Hibernian again this season in a pre-season friendly to mark the 50th anniversary of the event?

3 Which Hibernian player suffered broken ribs and a punctured lung in the first derby of the season?

4 In which country do Dnipro Dnipropetrovsk play?

5 Which Irish side did Hibernian play a friendly against in October?

6 How many times did Hibernian beat Rangers in the SPL this season?

7 Who won most SPL points in the derby encounters this season, Hibernian or Hearts?

Answers on page 60

Answers on page 60

www.hibernianfc.co.uk

HIBERNIAN
18 75
EDINBURGH

23

www.hibernianfc.co.uk

Rob Jones

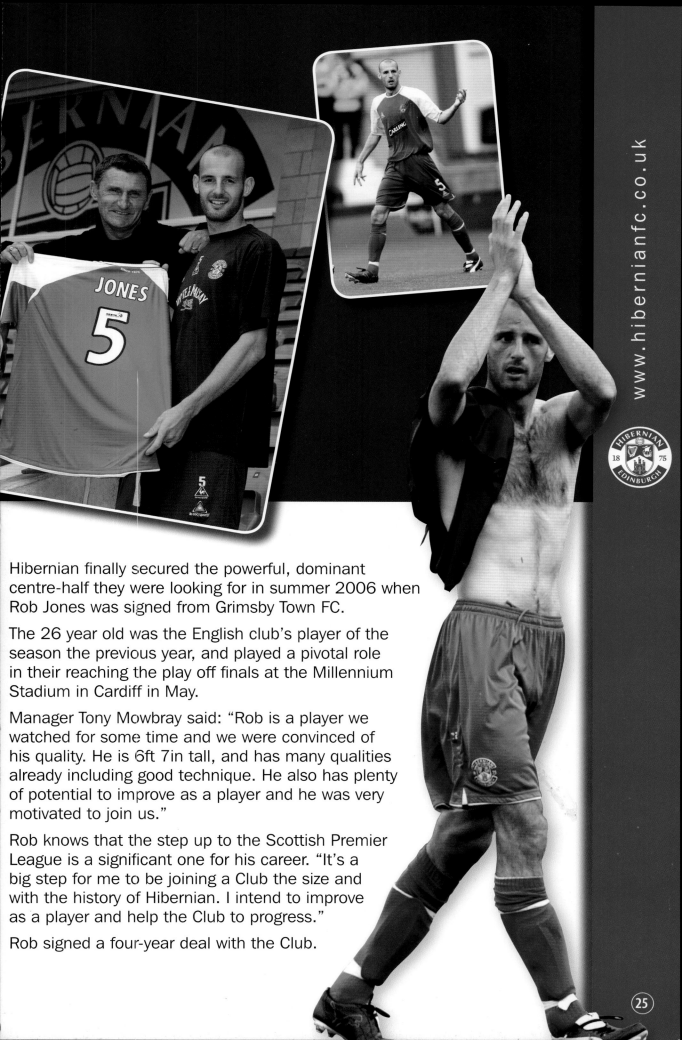

Hibernian finally secured the powerful, dominant centre-half they were looking for in summer 2006 when Rob Jones was signed from Grimsby Town FC.

The 26 year old was the English club's player of the season the previous year, and played a pivotal role in their reaching the play off finals at the Millennium Stadium in Cardiff in May.

Manager Tony Mowbray said: "Rob is a player we watched for some time and we were convinced of his quality. He is 6ft 7in tall, and has many qualities already including good technique. He also has plenty of potential to improve as a player and he was very motivated to join us."

Rob knows that the step up to the Scottish Premier League is a significant one for his career. "It's a big step for me to be joining a Club the size and with the history of Hibernian. I intend to improve as a player and help the Club to progress."

Rob signed a four-year deal with the Club.

No figure looms larger in the history of Hibernian in the post-war era than Eddie Turnbull. As player and manager, he was pivotal to the two greatest eras the Club has ever enjoyed and today rightly enjoys his status as the elder statesman of Scottish football.

As a player, Eddie was a part of the greatest forward line ever to wear the green-and-white of Hibernian, and arguably the greatest ever to grace Scottish or British football – the Famous Five.

Smith, Johnstone, Reilly, Turnbull, Ormond – the names still trip off the tongue of Hibernian fans too young by far ever to have seen the Five in action as they terrorised defences throughout Scotland and Europe, winning matches, trophies and plaudits along the way.

Eddie made his debut at Easter Road against Third Lanark on November 2nd, 1946 after he signed for the Club following his service on the Russian convoys in the Second World War. He, and his elder brother, were won over to Hibernian by the silver-tongued manager Willie McCartney.

Legend

Eddie was to enjoy an incredible career at Easter Road as part of the Famous Five, winning league championships, cups and becoming the first British player to score in European competition.

Eddie also represented his country, including playing in all three games in the 1958 finals when he was named one of the leading players in the tournament. He scored four goals against Manchester United in a friendly match, including one described by pundit and author Bob Crampsey as "one of the finest goals I have ever witnessed." Nor for nothing was Eddie known as "Thunderball".

A highlight of Eddie's playing career were the forays overseas, in particular as the first British Club participating in the European Cup. Eddie's name was first on the scoresheet as "we beat Rot-Weiss Essen 4-0 in Germany although they were not a bad team, with quite a few of the 1954 World Cup winning team in their ranks."

Hibernian were to go out to a brilliant Reims side inspired by one of

France's greatest-ever players, Raymond Kopa, in the semi finals. While the European Cup evokes great memories in Eddie, it also brings a little regret. By that time (1956) the Five were past their best. "If it had been a couple of years earlier, we'd have had a right good chance to win the Cup. At that time, we could have beat anyone on our day" said Eddie.

So how highly did Eddie rate the other four members of that fantastic forward line.

"Gordon Smith was fantastic, an artist. Every team in Scotland had good wingers in those days and he was the best. He had terrific skill in both feet, had great vision and was a fantastic passer of the ball. Bobby Johnstone was a silky player with tremendous vision, like Gordon. He could always see a pass and was great at linking the play.

"You can't teach people what Lawrie Reilly had. He never gave defenders a moments peace and he always knew how to be in the right place at the right time, a real strikers instinct. The final member was my wee pal Willie Ormond. He was one-footed, but what a foot it was. He was my room-mate on away trips, and my pal. If anyone touched Willie on the pitch I sorted them out."

Eddie played on Hibernian's tour of Brazil, another history-making event that saw the men in green-and-white create a stir with their intelligent, exciting attacking play. His final match for Hibernian was, appropriately in some ways, played overseas on a tour of Spain against Real Gijon in May 1959.

Once his playing days were over, he stayed on at Easter Road for a couple of years as trainer, then moving to Queens Park as trainer in 1961. He was asked to coach Scotland's amateurs to play in a tournament to mark the English FA's Centenary, and Eddie's side destroyed a German side coached by the great Helmut Schoen 5-2.

He then moved to Aberdeen to embark on his managerial career, called in to sort out the playing side of Pittodrie. Eddie carried out the task in typically blunt fashion, but within a short space of time had cleared out an old guard and brought in new, young exciting players.

"Way back in the mid '60s I was playing an 18-year-old Martin Buchan as a sweeper. I built my reputation as a

manager at Aberdeen at that time." Eddie's progress culminated in a Scottish Cup win in 1971, in a 3-1 win over Celtic in the final. Shortly afterwards, he was to return to his beloved Easter Road.

"I got the call soon after we won the Cup. I knew Tom Hart as a friend, and if it had been anybody else I might not have come back."

Eddie made a fantastic start at Easter Road, and in 1972 the team made the Scottish Cup final only to lose to the powerful Celtic side of Jock Stein by 6-1. "We got slaughtered, but I told them (the players) that we'd be back."

Soon afterwards, the same two sides met in the final of the League Cup, and this time Hibernian emerged victorious 5-3. Indeed, the team was unfortunate to be playing at the same time as the 9-in-a-row Celtic side led by Jock Stein which won the European Cup. If not for that dominance, greater success would surely have been achieved.

The team put together by Eddie in the 70s, Turnbulls Tornadoes, is still regarded as second only to the team of the Famous Five in terms of success, skill and entertainment.

Said Eddie: "I know that team still has a special place for a lot of people, especially because of the midfield and attack. But all the work began at the back with the goalie and back four, and that was the basis for everything we achieved."

Despite his prowess and his international recognition, Eddie was never awarded a Scotland cap. In those days, caps were awarded only in international matches against other Home Countries (England, Wales or Northern Ireland). It was entirely appropriate that, following intervention by Club Chairman Rod Petrie, Eddie should be finally honoured with the award of a commemorative Cap before a friendly international against Switzerland last March.

Eddie is still a regular at Hibernian matches, home and away, and is perfectly placed to give his own verdict on progress under Tony Mowbray. "He'll be a tough act to follow. He's got a good bunch of young players and he's got them trying to play the right way.

"I was always conscious of being an attack-minded footballing side. That's the Hibernian way, and you can tell that's Tony's philosophy. It's great to see talented youngsters like Steven Whittaker coming through the ranks along with Brown, Thomson and the rest. It all looks good."

Future wishes? Eddie says: "I am determined to see us win the Cup. It eluded the 70s team, and it even eluded the Famous Five. You need players with blood and thunder to stand up in a big Cup final, and a few times we let ourselves down. If I could see the Club win the Scottish Cup, I'd be the happiest of men."

www.hibernianfc.co.uk

HIBS UNVEIL TRAINING GROUN

Earlier this year Hibernian FC made an announcement that was music to the ears of the Club's players, coaches and supporters - solid progress in developing a training ground in East Lothian.

At the time of writing, the Club expected to have gained planning approval during the second half of the year, and the timetable was to be onsite as soon as possible with the centre available to be used as a base from pre-season this summer coming.

In making the announcement, the Club also shared its vision for the East Mains Training Centre for Hibernian FC. This will eventually include:

- **up to 10 full size grass pitches**
- **specialist training areas (eg goalkeeping)**
- **gym**
- **changing facilities**
- **a treatment area**
- **an indoor short-sided synthetic pitch**
- **players' lounge**
- **Coaches' rooms**

Once completed, the Club will own its own training facilities in perpetuity. At present, the Club utilises a portfolio of facilities around the city, and each year has sought to improve the quality of training facilities available to the Manager.

Tony Mowbray and the football management team have been involved in the development of the plans.

The early phase of works, including the purchase and the creation of a number of pitches and changing facilities is being funded from the Club's existing resources. The Club is also talking with supporter groups about fund-raising activities to help finance the wider project. In the past, at Club Listening Groups, supporters have shown a real willingness to raise funds for a tangible project for the long-term benefit of the Club.

Rod Petrie, Club Chairman, said: "The Board has made it our top priority to secure training facilities, and we are delighted to have taken this important step in doing so. It has been a long process, but at the end of the day securing the Club's own training facilities, fully within its ownership, is the ideal way ahead.

"We have secured the rights to a large area of land plus sizeable buildings and an existing infrastructure which offer us a lot of flexibility."

"However, while funding for an initial phase of the work is in place we will continue with the development over the coming few years to ensure that

LANS

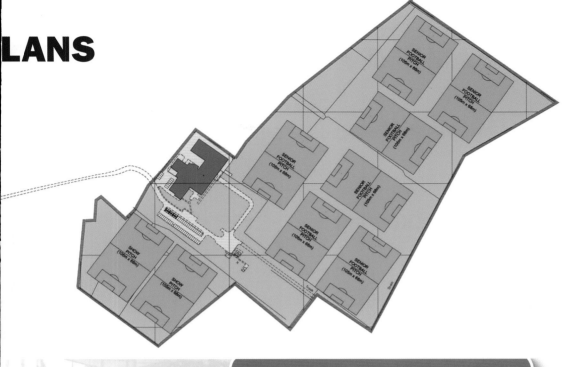

www.hibernianfc.co.uk

Hibernian has training facilities on a par with anything offered elsewhere. To do so, we will be exploring sources of funding including working closely with supporters in the months ahead to explore ways in which the creativity and ingenuity of supporters can help with future work."

Tony Mowbray, Manager, said: "I am delighted that the Club has taken this major step forward, which is significant progress. I have said many times that training facilities are, in my view, the number one priority. This development will mean that we will have a base to work from in producing better players and better teams. It is a very significant investment, and I am certain that in the years ahead it will prove to be money wisely spent as the Club continues to develop talented footballers."

The site is situated in East Lothian twenty minutes drive from Easter Road Stadium.

The Club's community and youth development activities will continue at a number of locations throughout Scotland, but will have access to East Mains Training Centre. The Club will remain based at Easter Road Stadium at the heart of its community.

Player Profiles

Goalkeepers:

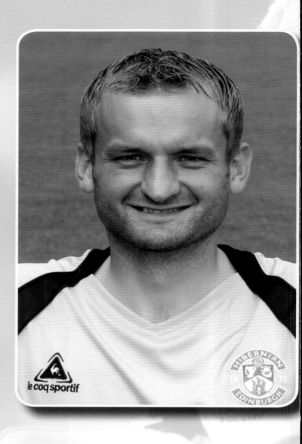

ZBIGNIEW MALKOWSKI
– goalkeeper

Born: 19 January 1978 in Poland

The keeper was signed from Dutch aces Feyenoord after appearing for the Club as a trialist in last season's pre-match tour of Ireland. A terrific shot-stopper, "Zibby" had established himself as Tony Mowbray's first choice 'keeper. He showed genuine character in putting in top-rate performances throughout the season.

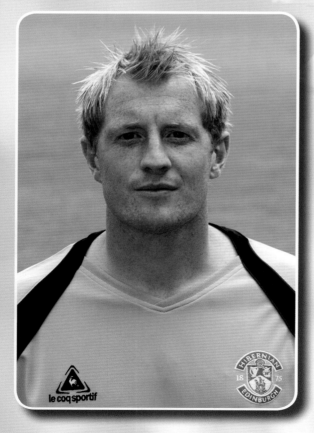

SIMON BROWN
– goalkeeper

Born: 3 December 1976 in Chelmsford

One of Tony Mowbray's first signings following the departure of goalies Nick Colgan and Daniel Anderson, Simon joined the Club from English league side Colchester. A burly 6ft 2in tall, Simon is an agile shot stopper and has been a regular first-team pick in league and Scottish Cup matches since making his debut in pre-season clashes with Cardiff City and Leeds United. Former clubs include Spurs, Fulham and Lincoln.

ALASTAIR BROWN
– goalkeeper

*Born: 12 December 1985
in Irvine*

Ally spent the season on loan with Raith Rovers. He made his first-team debut in the Intertoto Cup against Lithuanian side FK Vetra in season 2004/05 after Simon Brown was injured in training. He joined the Club in May 2003 from Cowdenbeath.

Defenders:

DAVID MURPHY
– defender

*Born: 1 March 1983
in Hartlepool*

David proved again to be one of the Club's most consistent performers and one of the outstanding left backs in Scottish football. He joined the Club in July 2004 when he came to the Club's attention's through the Manager's Middlesbrough connections. A powerful tackler, David brings strong defensive qualities to the side as well as being capable – as he has shown many times – of swashbuckling forays forward.

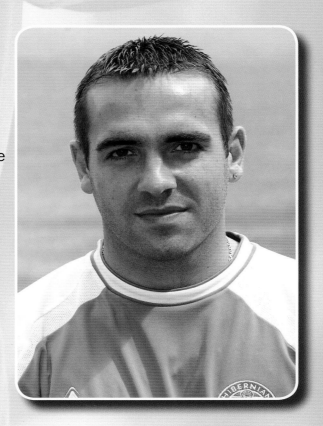

STEVEN WHITTAKER
– defender

*Born: 16 June 1984
in Edinburgh*

Steven proved his versatility during the season when he filled in for many games in midfield, and didn't look out of place in the team's engine room. His adventurous, athletic and skilful style of play has led to widespread acclaim and a host of under-21 caps. Dangerous and pacy with the ball at his feet, Steven is not afraid to have a crack at goal when the opportunity presents itself. Full international honours are a real target for this young player.

JONATHAN BAILLIE
– defender

Born: 2 September 1985 in Irvine

A young man who has suffered badly from injuries, Jonathan is another product of the highly-praised Hibernian youth system. He made his first-team debut in season 2003/04 in spectacular style, helping the team to a league cup quarter final win over Celtic by 2-1. Everyone hopes that this season can see him shake off his injury woes.

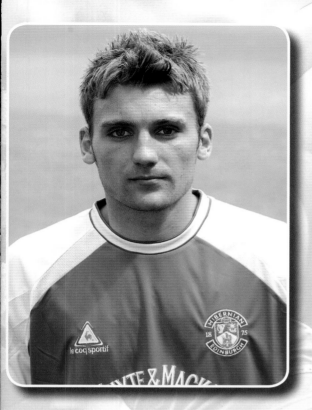

CHRIS HOGG
– defender

*Born: 12 March 1985
in Middlesbrough*

Chris played a significant role in the team last season after getting his chance through injuries and suspensions suffered by Gary Caldwell and Gary Smith. He took the opportunity well, and played in a high number of matches. Another Mowbray signing, Chris joined Hibernian from the Manager's previous Club Ipswich Town. A centre-back with great potential, Chris has represented England at various youth levels.

OUMAR KONDE
– defender

Born: 19 August 1979 in Switzerland

Oumar joined the Club in the transfer window in January 2006 from German side Hansa Rostock. An under 21 Swiss international, his pace and power have seen him play both in central defence and in a defensive midfield role. Previous clubs also include Premiership side Blackburn Rovers.

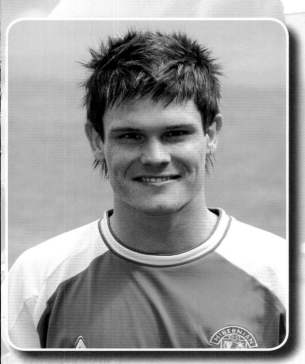

JAY SHIELDS – defender

Born: 6 July 1985 in Edinburgh

Came back into the side when Hibernian were struggling to cope with injuries towards the end of last season and let no-one down with some rousing performances. His whole-hearted commitment and aggression have been channelled into a positive force, and he has improved as a footballer as a result.

Midfield:

SCOTT BROWN
– midfield

Born: 25 June 1985 in Fife

A player who just seems to get better and better as each month goes by and last season he impressed in a mature midfield role despite a serious injury suffered in a derby at Tynecastle. Scott has a fantastic ability to cover the ground, can score with either foot, and is capable of making exciting and dangerous runs – but he is also prepared to work for the team and doesn't neglect his defensive duties. Scott gained full international status last season. He was sorely missed by the team during his period on the sidelines.

GUILLAUME BEUZELIN
– midfield

Born: 14 April 1979 in Le Havre, France

Another of the highly prized midfielders at Easter Road who missed much of the season past through injury, Guillaume will be hoping for better luck this season. A quality midfield player skilled on either foot and with a superb first touch, Guillaume is an integral part of Tony Mowbray's determination to play passing, attacking football. His ability to make the best use of space and to see a pass early has been a major source of excitement around Easter Road. And he can score, as well. Guillaume joined from Le Havre.

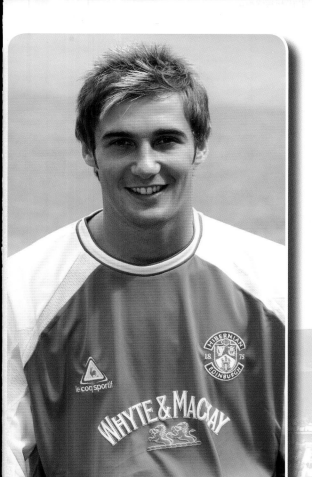

KEVIN THOMSON
– midfield

*Born: 16 January 1983
in Edinburgh*

Another talented midfielder, Kevin had to shoulder much of the responsibility for running the Hibernian midfield in the absences of Messrs Beuzelin, Brown and Stewart through injury last season.

A real talent, with a gifted left-foot Kevin is a firm favourite with all Hibernian fans and is being widely touted as a full international in the near future.

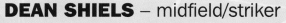

DEAN SHIELS – midfield/striker

Born: 1 February 1985 in Northern Ireland

Dean's season was also hit hard by long-term injury – in his case one that told a remarkable story. Dean has been blind in one eye since a freak accident at the age of eight and has managed a career in top flight football despite it. When the condition of the injured eye deteriorated so much last season that it caused pain and discomfort he required surgery to have it removed. Dean was back training and playing at the end of the season – ahead of schedule! Dean joined the Club from Arsenal.

STEPHEN GLASS
– midfield/defender

*Born: 23 May 1976
in Dundee*

A left-sided player of real quality, Stephen moved to Hibernian at the start of season 2003/04 from Watford. He plays a key role in both midfield and, when required, as cover at full-back. His versatility and consistency saw Stephen rewarded with an extended contract. His former Clubs include Aberdeen and Newcastle United.

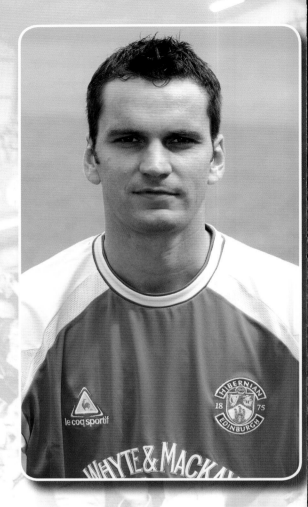

IVAN SPROULE
– midfield

*Born: 18 February 1981
in Omagh, Northern Ireland*

Blistering pace persuaded Tony Mowbray to take a chance on Ivan, who joined Hibernian from Irish side Institute. He produced the moment of the season for Hibernian fans when he came on as a substitute to score a hat-trick in a 3-0 league win at Ibrox against Rangers. Ivan looks set to provide many moments of excitement for Easter Road fans in the years ahead after signing an extended contract.

MICHAEL STEWART
– midfield

Born: 26 February 1981 in Edinburgh

Michael is one of a handful of players who has turned out for both Edinburgh clubs, having signed for Hibernian following a one-year spell at Hearts, where he was on loan from Manchester United. The talented playmaker sees the tutelage of Tony Mowbray as key to kick-starting a career that saw him turn out for the Red Devils in the Champions League. Can play a big role for Hibernian this term.

JAMIE MCCLUSKEY
– midfield

Born: 6 November 1987 in Bellshill

"Jinky" is a lively, talented little player who has huge potential. A box of tricks and feints he is an old-fashioned crowd-pleaser. Undoubtedly the best is still to come from this star in the making.

ANTONIO MURRAY
– midfield

Born: 15 September 1984 in Cambridge

Antonio suffered from long-term back problems last season that saw him play a restricted role for the Club. He was signed from Ipswich Town. The son of Italian and Scottish parents, brought up in England's south east, he has a decent touch, strong shot and is fearless in the tackle.

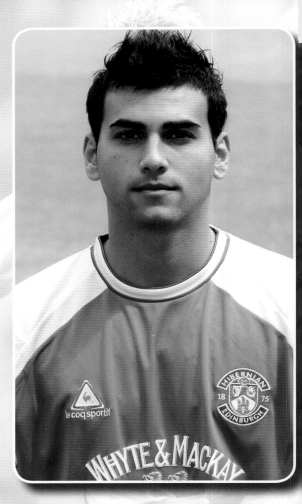

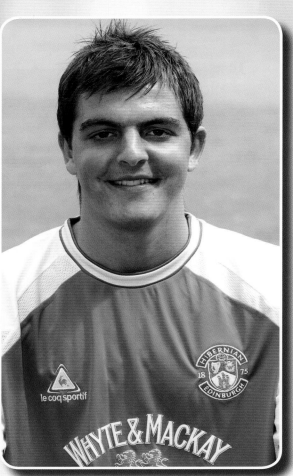

KEVIN MCDONALD
– midfield

Born: 26 June 1985 in Newcastle-upon-Tyne

"Geordie" is a talented young footballer who has the potential to develop into a first-team regular. He has excellent passing ability and can score goals and will be hoping that this is the season when he can finally make the breakthrough.

Strikers:

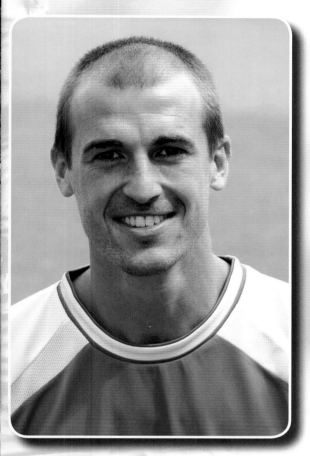

PAUL DALGLISH
– striker/midfield

Born: 18 February 1977 in Glasgow

Paul joined Hibernian from then SPL rivals Livingston and has proven to be a hard-working player who can perform in midfield, out wide or up front. He brings experience, talent and hard work to every match he plays.

CHRIS KILLIN
– striker

Born: 8 October 1981 in New Zealand

The burly 6ft Kiwi international got off to a storming start after joining Hibernian in the January transfer window in 2006, scoring four goals in six starts and bringing a predator's instinct to a team Manager Tony Mowbray wanted to see score "more scruffy goals." Injury brought his season to a premature end, and he will be hoping for a good run in the team to help his goals tally grow. He signed from Oldham, and also spent time with Manchester City.

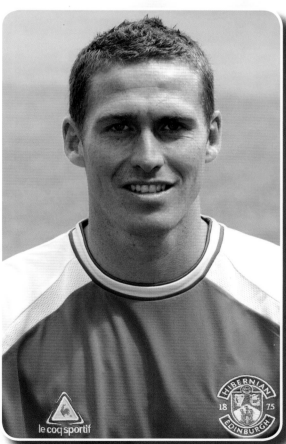

SAM MORROW
– striker

*Born: 3 March 1985
in Londonderry, Northern Ireland*

Signed in the summer of 2004 from Ipswich Town, Sam has not had the chances at Easter Road he would have wished for due to the form of team-mates. He spent much of last season on loan to Livingston, before being injured at the end of the campaign. He will be hoping this season brings better fortune.

STEVEN FLETCHER
– striker

*Born: 26 March 1987
in Shrewsbury*

Perhaps the outstanding young striker in the SPL, Steven has won acclaim from critics and fans alike for the quality of his performances for the first-team – when asked to play up front or in a midfield role. His non-stop style and his ability on the ball mark him out as a young player with the ability to make it at the very top as ten goals in the last campaign testify. A key performer for the Scotland U-19 side also.

AMADOU KONTE
– striker

Born: 23 January 1981 in Mali

A quick, strong centre-forward Amadou Konte added some real physical presence to Hibernian's goal threat when he signed in January 2005 from Cambridge United. A towering 6ft 3in tall, he has also played at Strasbourg and at FC Porto, Villanovense (in Spain) and in Italy at Serie C1 side Paterno Calcio.

ABDESSALEM BENJELLOUN
– striker

Born: 28 January 1985 in Morocco

"Benji" joined the Club in March 2006 following several weeks of behind-the-scenes work to secure the Moroccan under-21 international a work permit. The 21-year-old has tremendous talent, and Tony Mowbray has high hopes for him. Benji immediately became a hit with Hibernian fans, scoring the winner in a 2-1 derby win against Hearts at Easter Road.

Club History and Honours

Hibernian FC was founded in 1875 by members of the Catholic Young Men's Society attached to St Patrick's Church in Edinburgh's "Little Ireland" – the Cowgate.

The name – decided on by Canon Edward Hannan and the Club's first captain and co-founder Michael Whelahan – derives from the Latin and means Irishmen.

Playing in green and white, the Club quickly established a reputation for its play and won the Scottish Cup in 1887 thanks to a 2-1 win over Dumbarton.

Hibernian was the first British Club to play in European competition in season 1955/56, the first to play under floodlights and to install under-soil heating and – in the 1980s – broke the mould by allowing shirt sponsorship. In the past season, the Club scored another first by including sponsorship on its shorts.

Periods of great success have blossomed throughout the Club's history –Championships delivered in 1902/03 and in 1947/48 with a further one in 1950/51 and again the following season – the peak of powers of the Club's most celebrated team dominated by arguably the greatest forward line the British domestic game has seen, "The Famous Five."

The Scottish game's other major prize, the Scottish Cup, has been won only twice – first of all in 1887 and again in 1902 in a 1-0 win over Celtic. League Cup wins have been achieved more recently in 1972/73 and again in 1991/92.

The first of these wins was achieved during the Club's second golden era – that of Turnbull's Tornadoes.

Sir Tom Farmer CBE saved the Club in 1991 when its owner, the listed company Forth Investments plc, went into receivership. The new stability brought to the Club paid immediate dividends to the fans when Hibernian won the 1991 Skol League Cup, beating Rangers in the semi finals (1-0) and Dunfermline in the final (2-0).

The mid 1990s saw the building of two new stands giving Easter Road an all covered capacity of 16,000 seats, and at the turn of the decade we bid farewell to the famous Easter Road slope, and the construction of a magnificent new main stand took capacity to more than 17,000.

Tony Mowbray's arrival two seasons ago has seen a resurgence in the Club's tradition for playing exciting, passing football and the emergence of some of Scotland's finest young players at Easter Road.

www.hibernianfc.co.uk

HONOURS & REWARDS

FOUNDED:	1875
Scottish League Winners(4)	1902/03, 1947/48, 1950/51, 1951/52
First Division winners (2)	1980/81, 1998/99
Division Two winners (3)	1893/94, 1894/95, 1932/33
Division One runners-up (6)	1896/97, 1946/47, 1949/50, 1952/53, 1973/74, 1974/75
Scottish Cup winners (2)	1887, 1902
Scottish Cup runners-up (9)	1896, 1914, 1923, 1924, 1947, 1958, 1972, 1979, 2001
Scottish League Cup winners (2)	1972/73, 1991/92
Scottish League Cup runners-up (5)	1950/51, 1968/69, 1974/75, 1985/86, 1993/94
Drybrough Cup winners (2)	1972/73, 1973/74
Summer Cup winners (2)	1941, 1964
European Cup	six matches (best: semi-final 1955/56)
Cup Winners' Cup	six matches (best: third round 1972/73)
UEFA/Fairs Cup	60 matches (best: semi-final Fairs Cup 1960/61)
Record Home Attendance	65,860 versus Heart of Midlothian, January 2 1950
Most Capped Player	Lawrie Reilly, 38, Scotland
Most League Appearances	Arthur Duncan, 446
Most League goals scored in a season by an individual	Joe Baker, 42, 1959/60 season
Most goals scored by an individual (all seasons)	Gordon Smith, 364

RECORD VICTORIES

All Matches	22-1 versus 42nd Highlanders, September 3 1881
League Home win	11-1 versus Hamilton Academical, Nov 6 1965;
Away win	11-1 versus Airdrie, October 24 1959
Premier Division	8-1 versus Kilmarnock, April 2 1983
Scottish Cup	15-1 versus Peebles Rovers, February 11 1961
League Cup	11-2 versus Alloa, September 22 1965
Europe	9-1 versus Rosenborg Trondheim, UEFA Cup, Oct 2 1974

Four seasons have seen the top league championship delivered to Hibernian FC.

The first, in season 1902/03, was achieved through accumulating 37 points from 22 games (remember, in those days it was two points for a win and one for a draw). The team's only defeat of the season was suffered at Third Lanark. That season, the Club also won the East of Scotland Shield and the Rosebery Charity Cup. Liverpool were defeated during a trip to England. The previous season, the team had won the Scottish Cup, the Rosebery Charity Cup and the Glasgow Charity Cup.

These were two of the Club's greatest seasons, enjoyed under the stewardship of one Dan McMichael who was treasurer, secretary and Manager.

The second championship was delivered in season 1947/48. The league season kicked off on a Wednesday afternoon at Pittodrie with over 40,000 crammed into the ground, hundreds sitting on the roof of the stand, to see Hibernian record a 2-0 win with goals from Gordon Smith and Eddie Turnbull.

1951/52 League Championship-winning side, ir

1951/52 League Championship-winning side, including the 'Famous Five' sitting in the front row.

Willie McCartney.

That season also saw the emergence of a young Lawrie Reilly, who stood in for centre-forward Alec Linwood against Queen of the South when he was stricken with flu. Reilly scored a hat-trick in a 6-0 win. Hibernian suffered only two further defeats before the turn of the year, and rattled up a string of victories including an 8-0 demolition of Third Lanark with five goals from Gordon Smith and an Alec Linwood hat-trick. As the year ended, Hibernian were lying second from top behind Partick Thistle.

Hibernian then beat Hearts 3-1 in the New Year's derby at Easter Road. Within a few weeks the mood changed, with the death of popular manager Willie McCartney. He was succeeded by Hugh Shaw. Rangers, by now leading the table, were the first to visit Easter Road following McCartney's death and Hibernian won a hard-fought match to move within one point of their rivals.

A strong run of form saw Hibernian take a three point lead over Rangers, with the Ibrox men having two games in hand. In the next round of games, Hibernian beat Celtic at Parkhead while Rangers lost to Queens Park. Hibernian then destroyed Motherwell 5-0 at home, leaving Rangers

ing the 'Famous Five' sitting in the front row.

Lawrie Reilly.

needing to win their final three games, scoring 26 goals and conceding 0 to snatch the league. The best Rangers could manage was a 1-1 draw with Motherwell and the title was Hibernian's.

McCartney had laid the foundations for the great Famous Five team of the 1950s, and Hugh Shaw made the finest use of them. Smith, Johnstone, Reilly, Turnbull and Ormond were the mainstays although the team contained many other fine players.

These included Bobby Combe, who often deputised for any member of the Five when injured.

The league championships were claimed in seasons 1950/51 and again in 1951/52, and were within a whisker in claiming runners up spot the following year, losing out to Rangers on goal average – had it been decided by modern goal difference methods Hibernian would have claimed the title. Rangers and Hibernian both achieved 43 points that year.

In season 50/51 Hibernian won the title with 48 points, the following season with 46.

During this period, Rangers provided the main opposition, and their success was built on a rock-like defence nicknamed The Iron Curtain. Many pundits have expressed the view that Scotland's selectors could have done worse than pick the Rangers defence and the Hibernian forward line. A combination of the Iron Curtain and the Famous Five would have made a fascinating line-up, but it was never to be.

New Moroccan Star for Easter Road

Moroccan playmaker Merouane Zemmama signed a five-year deal at the club following the awarding of a work permit in August.

Zemmama spent five weeks training at Easter Road in order to impress the coaching staff, and he certainly achieved that with Manager Tony Mowbray expressing great delight at the signing.

Zemmama at just 22-years-old does little to raise the average age of a still very young Hibernian side, but he is a player that Tony Mowbray refers to in enthusiastic – but cautionary - terms: "It's important not to build him up too much - people have to be prepared to let him settle into our way of life and our football but his talent will be evident."

Perhaps the most telling summation of his signing came when the manager likened Zemmama in style to one of the players who gave so much enjoyment to Hibernian supporters in recent years, Russell Latapy: "He can score wonderful free-kicks and although he is a pretty diminutive character, he's shown in training he doesn't lack a heart or determination

"When I look at him, he is a Russell Latapy-type player. But he can run fast and long and get himself about the pitch as well as having all the technique and skill."

Magic Moment

August 27th, 2005 was a day that will be forever etched into the memory of the small army of travelling Hibernian fans who journeyed through to Ibrox for a league encounter with Rangers.

The two sides had cancelled each other out for the first hour of the match, when Tony Mowbray made an inspired substitution and pushed on speedy striker Ivan Sproule.

The Ulsterman ran the tiring Rangers defence ragged, striking in the 67th minute to give Hibernian a lead before breaking away to score twice in the final five minutes to seal a famous win that received praise from fans and players alike as the season's "Magic Moment."

QUIZ

HISTORY QUIZ

1. When was the Club founded?

2. What does the name Hibernian mean?

3. How many times has the Club won the league championship?

4. Who is the most-capped Hibernian player ever?

5. What was the name of the most successful Hibernian forward line?

6. Which French internationalist captained Hibernian in a Scottish Cup Final?

7. Which former Hibernian star was selected for Trinidad & Tobago during the 2006 World Cup finals?

8. Who defeated Hibernian in the Scottish Cup semi final last season?

Answers on page 61

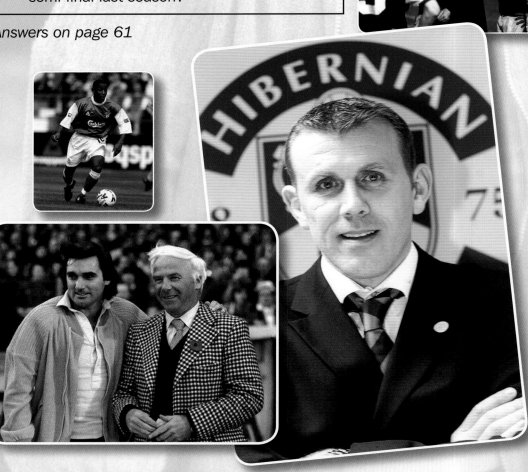

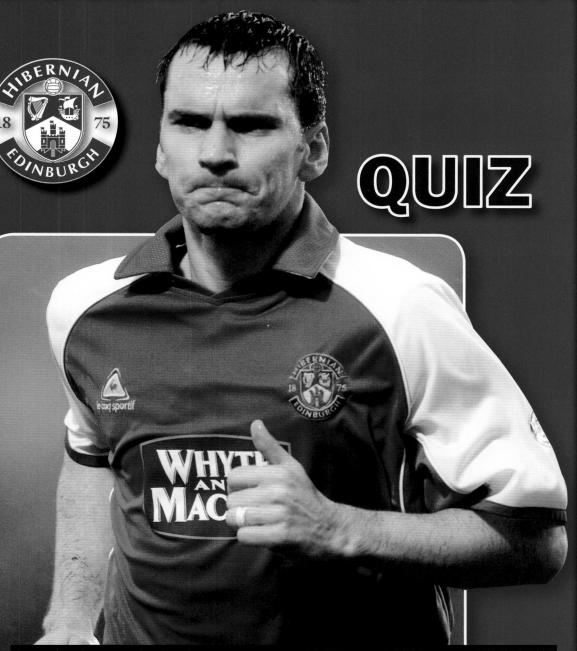

QUIZ

Which Hibernian players are/were known by the following nicknames:

1.	Sloop	
2.	Yogi	
3.	Kaiser	
4.	Sodjer	
5.	The Quiet Man	
6.	Thunderball	
7.	Broonaldo	

Answers on page 60

HIBS KIDS

Hibs Kids is the official Hibernian supporters club for Under 14's.

Membership in the past two years has increased to over 3,000 Hibs Kids, proving it's one of the best young supporters clubs in Scotland. For just £10 per year, members can look forward to the following Hibee benefits:

Keep in touch with...

- A regular Hibs Kids Newsletter, featuring the latest news, reviews, and competitions.

- Birthday Card for your special day.

Your chance to attend the following events...

- Hibs Kids Days at Easter Road Stadium with season ticket holders able to 'bring a friend' for £5

- Hibs Kids Christmas events.

- Discounts to Hibernian's Holiday Soccer Schools for children aged 5-12.

- Free access to SPL Reserve fixtures at Easter Road.

Look forward to more benefits including...

- 5-11 years old are entered free into Mascot Draw for home game.

- 11-14 years old entered into a Ball Person Draw.

- Discounted rate to attend 'Footie4Kid's – Hibernian's new community coaching programme.

To join please call the Ticket Office on Tel: 0131 661 1875. Alternatively visit the Club website www.hibernianfc.co.uk and follow the "Supporters" link.

InterToto Cup

When the final whistle blew on July 22nd at the end of a pulsating 90 minutes the story was all too familiar to Scottish football fans – an heroic performance, a terrific home win, but an exit from European competition on the away goals rule.

Hibernian enjoyed a titanic struggle over two legs with Danish outfit Odense, and also one or two entertaining little side issues. The Danes were captained by a former Easter Road Great Dane, Ulrik Laursen, who was to play a pivotal role at centre back over both legs, and were also managed by Scot Bruce Rioch – once Tony Mowbray's boss and mentor at Middlesbrough.

The locking of Viking horns had an added piquancy then, but with great good nature and mutual respect.

In Denmark, Hibernian lost 1-0 to a hotly disputed penalty, with TV evidence clearly backing up full-back David Murphy's assertions that a last-ditch tackle had been fair with the ball won cleanly. The goal however, stood, and a couple of missed chances were to come back to haunt Hibernian.

The return leg at Easter Road was initially balanced on a knife edge, but when the Danes were first to score early in the second half Hibernian were left with a mountain to climb. But a quick riposte from Rob Jones with 35 minutes remaining was followed by a Dalglish strike to set up a thundering final ten minutes. However it was not to be.

The previous round was a hugely different story, with Hibernian crushing Latvian side Dinaburg Daugavpils 8-0 on aggregate – a 5-0 home hammering followed by a professional 3-0 away win in Eastern Europe.

AYRES

Year to Push On

John Park has helped nurture a multitude of talents now regularly gracing Hampden Park as Scotland internationalists from his time at Hibernian and, before that, Motherwell.

As Academy Director John has seen the emergence of a crop of current first team stars including Scott Brown, Kevin Thomson, Steven Fletcher, and Steven Whittaker – all four named in the Scotland under 21 set up and Scott Brown already a full internationalist also.

He's also seen players such as Riordan and O'Connor come through the ranks of his youth system, so when he pinpoints a couple of youngsters to watch during the coming year it is worth listening in.

"I like to think that each year we will see a couple of the young lads start to force their way into the Manager's thoughts and challenge for a place in the first team squad.

"During the coming year I think we will see that continue, and in particular I will be looking for Ross Campbell and Keegan Ayres to mount a real challenge.

"In itself that is quite interesting, because the boys have come via different routes that illustrate what we try to achieve at this Club.

ACADEMY
TWO TO WATCH

"Ross is a bright, lively young striker who is a contemporary of Steven Fletcher and is now starting to show the kind of consistent good form that has already earned him a call up or two for the first team. Fans will remember he scored the winner in the pre-season friendly against Premiership side Charlton. He's come up through the ranks here, and it has been terrific to see him develop and if he keeps working hard the rewards will come.

"Keegan is a clever, skilful midfielder. He is a Canadian lad, who spent much of his time developing as a player over there. But we cast our net far and wide in searching for good young talent, and he is someone who we ran the rule over and liked.

"Our job has been to further his development and hone his talents further, and he is developing into a very good midfielder.

"These lads qualify for the under 19 team, but both know that if they are good enough they will get their chance at Easter Road. Our reputation for developing good young players and giving them a real chance to make it to the first team is helping us attract good talent, and these boys are excellent examples."

Celebrity Fans

Hibernian has always been the kind of Club that attracts more than its share of weel-kent faces. Today is no exception, with the Club's database including a fair smattering of famous fans.

Some, of course, make no secret of their allegiance – such as author Irvine Welsh, singers The Proclaimers, and radio presenter Grant Stott. However one man can make a legitimate claim to being Hibernian's best-known celebrity fan – actor Dougray Scott.

Dougray, star of Hollywood movies such as Mission Impossible II and Enigma, is a season ticket holder who makes it to as many matches as his busy schedule allows, and is always happy to do what he can to raise awareness of the Club.

Indeed, mention of his devotion to the Club peppers many an interview. In one, he told a journalist for the Observer:

"I was brought up with great Hibs teams of the past, like the Famous Five Team. It's unbelievable now but Hibs reached the semi-final of the first-ever European Cup in 1956...

"I grew up watching a phenomenal team in the 70s that included really good players such as John Blackley, Alan Gordon, Jimmy O'Rourke and John Brownlie. They were called Turnbull's Tornadoes after the manager, Eddie Turnbull. They played a version of total football that the Dutch were famous for."

He goes on: "Football conjures up a greater range of emotions for me than what I do. Acting doesn't get me as passionate. Don't get me wrong – I love acting and I take my work incredibly seriously, and I'm an acting animal in one sense. But I'm more of a football animal, not in a hooligan sense, but in what it does for me. If I had a choice of an evening with Robert De Niro or Sir Alex Ferguson it would be Alex Ferguson every time.

"And if it was a choice between Hibs winning the Premier League or me winning an Oscar, I'd rather Hibs won the title."

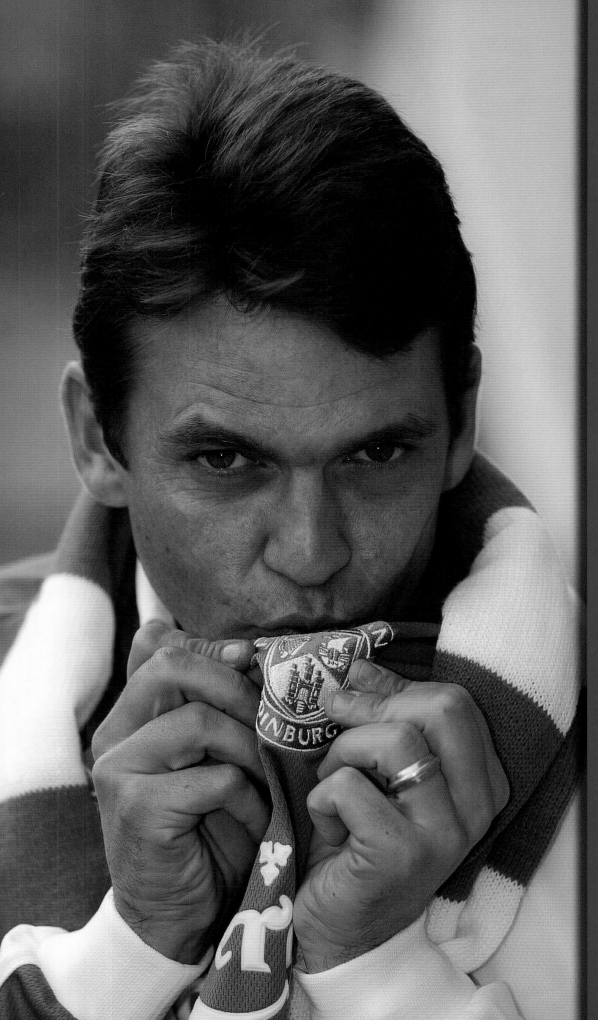

57

SKIPPER

The choice of classy midfielder Kevin Thomson to captain the Club this season may have caught one or two pundits on the hop – but the under 21 international was the man the Manager asked to provide leadership on the pitch.

Kevin is one of the youngest captains in the Club's history, but is determined that he will also go down as one of the finest.

He took over from central defender Gary Caldwell following his move to Celtic. Kevin said: " I am not big on shouting and moaning at the players around me but I hope I can lead by example and show that I can help the team.

"It is a huge honour to be asked to be Captain, and to be honest I was a bit surprised but when I thought about it I knew I had to say yes."

"It's a great honour to be asked to captain a top team like Hibernian, and I am fully aware of just how much this Club means to everyone associated with it."

Kevin promised that he will do everything he can to ensure that the free-flowing, attacking football that has delighted fans and pundits alike during the past two seasons will again be much in evidence.

He said: "The style of football we try to play wins us a lot of plaudits but it also really suits me as a player, so I am delighted. It's good that the Club strengthened in a couple of areas to increase competition for places, because competition is healthy and keeps players on their toes and performing and in my own position in midfield we have a lot of talented players so I know I have to keep performing, Captain or not, to be assured of my place. That goes for all of the players.

"As ever, we will be aiming to finish as high up the league as we can. As well as tackling the Old Firm, we also have to be prepared to meet the challenge that big-spending Hearts now pose to all the other Clubs but there is no reason why we should not be up for that. We have shown that in one-off games we can be a match for anyone in the country.

"The fans play a big part in making our season, and they have been fantastic the last two seasons, turning up in big numbers home and away with several sell-outs at Easter Road really helping to spur us on. I would urge them to carry on being our twelfth man at Easter Road, helping us turn our ground into a fortress, and making sure we know they are right behind us all the time. It really helps!"

TALKS

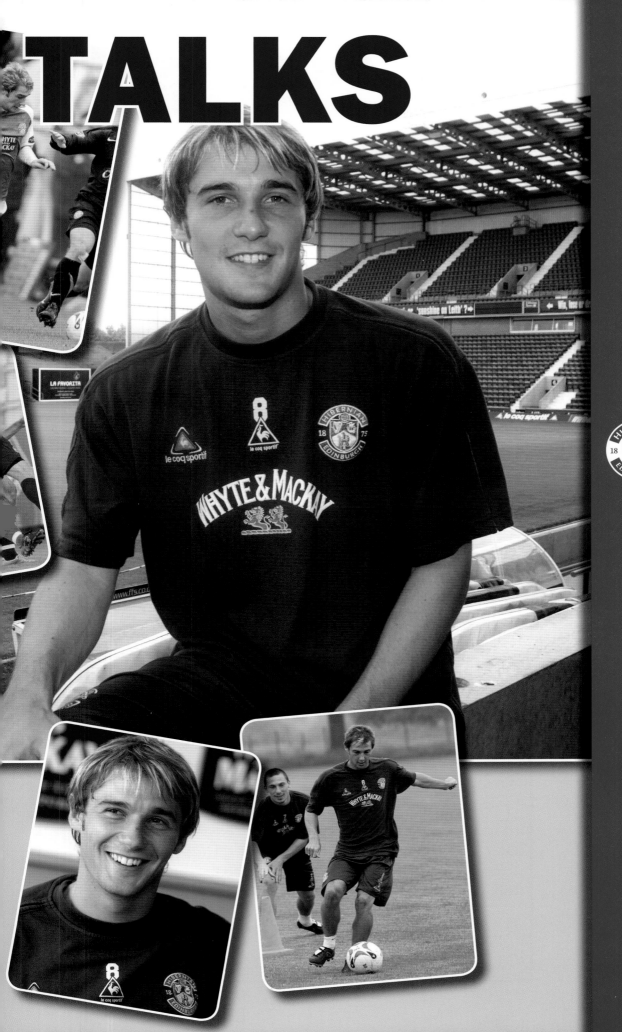

QUIZ ANSWERS

Quiz of the Season

1. **THREE**

2. **ROT-WEISS ESSEN**

3. **GARY CALDWELL**

4. **UKRAINE**

5. **INSTITUTE**

6. **TWICE**

7. **EACH CLUB GAINED SIX POINTS, WINNING THEIR HOME DERBIES**

NICKNAMES

Which Hibernian players are/were known by the following nicknames:		
1.	Sloop	JOHN BLACKLEY
2.	Yogi	JOHN HUGHES
3.	Kaiser	FRANCK SAUZEE
4.	Sodjer	ALEX CROPLEY
5.	The Quiet Man	PAT STANTON
6.	Thunderball	EDDIE TURNBULL
7.	Broonaldo	SCOTT BROWN

HISTORY QUIZ

1. **1875**

2. **IRISHMEN (MEN OF IRELAND)**

3. **FOUR**

4. **LAWRIE REILLY**

5. **FAMOUS FIVE**

6. **SAUZEE**

7. **RUSSELL LATAPY**

8. **HEARTS**

www.hibernianfc.co.uk

Staying in Contact With Your Club

There are a number of ways of keeping abreast with what is happening at your Club. These include visiting the website on www.hibernianfc.co.uk and also subscribing to our weekly e-mail newsletter, which can be done through visiting the website and clicking on the "News" link and then following the instructions given.

The Club is based at:

**Easter Road Stadium,
12 Albion Place,
Edinburgh EH7 5QG**

Telephone 0131 661 2159.